On Fear a

A P

Noa

Fear and Faith

Many people are "born into" mental slavery, to quote Bob Marley, but once they reach the age of maturity they are as responsible for their beliefs as their parents were when they first came of age. Familiarity with fear is not an excuse for choosing to live in it after being faced with the realities of a world governed in large part by fear and faith, even less so when that person has been reasonably educated and knows the difference between reason and faith. Are the adults of our world lost forever from the grasp of reason and intellectual freedom? Perhaps you think that with greater age it would be easier to use an appeal to reason and sanity in regards to the argument against religion. You would sadly be mistaken. Whenever I think of the problem of freeing grown minds in the thrall of fear I remember a conversation I had once with a young evangelical Christian. This was perhaps a year ago, and I was sitting in the common room of my residence hall reading a book. There was a group of young people animatedly talking on a set of couches about 20 feet to my left. One of this group (a young man I will call John) walked over to me and politely enquired as to what I was reading. I told him that it was a book about the intellectual and religious origins of creationism. A look of quite excitement crept across his face. He asked what I thought about creationism. It was at this point that I realized that John was a Christian.

The subtle tone of religious fervor had crept into his voice, and I could see that his eyes had begun to glaze over as if lost in another conversation entirely. I told him that I was interested in the topic in a purely academic sense. I mentioned that I subscribed to the idea that creationism was merely a pseudo-science created in order to better combat evolutionary theory. I saw an immediate reaction in John. He suddenly moved closer, smiled broadly and asked me why

I thought creationism was a pseudo-scientific idea. Relishing the idea of an intelligent conversation I answered that I thought that creationism was not valid because it was not testable in a scientific sense and that it derived from religious doctrine and not from actual observation of the real world. I also told him that I was not an expert in the field at all, but that I found science fascinating. I asked him what he thought about the idea of evolution. Things took an odd turn from this point onwards. Instead of directly answering my question John said that he thought the idea of evolution was "intriguing".

He then went off in a completely different direction and started to tell me about the success he had achieved with his various business endeavors. I was struck by this. John was avoiding the question entirely and was instead trying to impress me with a well-rehearsed story about his financial prowess. I felt like I was on the receiving end of a sales pitch. I would soon find out that my feeling was accurate. Finished with his story John then asked me what I was majoring in. I told him that I was majoring in history. He reacted positively to that and told me that he was interested in history also. It was at this point that the conversation lagged a bit and John wandered off to talk to his friends. I continued reading, but about five minutes later John returned with a look of purpose and excitement on his face. He asked me what religion I was. It was my turn to smile. I put down my book, and I told him that I was an Atheist. John looked stunned. This was the only moment of the entire conversation that I felt I was looking at a genuine human being.

He let down his guard for one moment then, and I saw his eyes widen, his breath quicken, and his jaw go slightly slack. This lapse only lasted a moment however before the rigid smile came across his face again, and his eyes glazed over. His moment had come. He knelt down to my level, peered into my eyes, and told me he was a Christian. He then asked me if I had ever read the Bible? I told him that I had read some of it before. Not missing a beat he asked me what I had thought of it? I responded as polite as I could manage that I thought there were many beautiful parts of it, but that it did not make much of an impression on me overall. John then proceeded to finally answer my earlier question about evolution. What follows is my best recollection of what he said:

"I believe in the truth of God's words in the Bible. I believe that the Bible gives the correct version of the creation of the world. I am God's creation, as are you. He loves us all with all of his heart. What do you think of that?" I leaned in a little closer to him. He recoiled a bit, and I could tell that he was sweating. "I think that I have no more reason to believe that your God created me then I would to believe that I was created by Thor or Vishnu. Nothing I have ever seen in this world has ever led me to believe that I was created in the image of anything." John slowly shook his head. He looked a little sad, but also looked as if he had expected my answer. He whispered under his breath "But... The love and the heart...".

I looked into his eyes at this moment and I saw nothing staring back at me. His eyes were empty, glazed like a piece of pottery. His face was a mask covering a shivering, tearful, terrified child who could not escape the intellectual cage into which it had been placed. I felt an incredibly sense of compassion and pity for this person under the mask, and I wished that I could talk to this hidden personage if only for a moment. This moment passed however, and John stood up. He told me that his friends and he were part of a youth ministry, and that I was welcome to come to one of their meetings if I wanted to. We shook hands, and he left to talk with his friends again. It was as if nothing had ever happened. Why did I tell this story? I feel that it is one of the best examples of how religion impacts the life and thought of an individual. John was articulate, obviously intelligent, and very likable. But talking to him was like talking to a well programmed robot: he did not seem to be able to understand the world outside of his narrow Christian world view. I was not a person to him: I was a soul to be collected, a mind to be conquered, a vessel into which that foul brew called fear could be poured, and nothing more. John represents the state of a large percentage of our population today. We live amongst the walking wounded of a war that is wagged every day in the churches, the schools, and the living rooms of our entire nation. I sometimes feel that I am walking within an invisible prison. This is a subtle prison: the walls cannot always be felt, and the bars can even be comforting. 90% of the world resides within this prison, and most were born into it. There is a sense of community within these hidden walls. A family of necessity is formed to cope with the pain and the fear of religious life. As with many families there are parents. These parents exercise control over the other members of the family unit. They were of course children once themselves, and their actions are largely explained by this fact, but this does not reduce their culpability in the abuse they inflict upon the new generation of prisoners. These are the parents, the teachers, the preachers, the leaders, and the saints of our society. We must be aware of this sorrowful fact if we are to survive the coming cataclysm.

Faith is the syringe that plunges the poison of fear into our veins. Marx insinuated that faith was the drug of choice for humanity. This is not the case; faith is the means fear has to achieving its end; that of consuming and usurping the human potential for reason and imagination. Faith is a vessel for fear, and perhaps the chief vessel. Faith teaches us nothing more than to fear our world, our bodies, our passions, and our minds. When we look out a high window our minds want to see a beautiful panorama of images and ideas and potential. What faith makes our minds see is a deadly fall from a dangerous place; a place to be avoided. Faith has for thousands of generations shuttered our windows upon the world, and closed our minds to the wonderful symphony of enlightening ideas.

Instead we are made to sit trussed and mute before an altar, and listen aptly to a cacophony of fear. When we hear a prayer we are told that we are listening to a communication with god. What we are in fact listening to is a terrified fool muttering reassurances to himself in the face of darkness. This darkness is the shadow of an imagined hulk; a Gollum created by humanity to protect itself from its own dynamic mind. Why did humanity feel the need to so strenuously protect itself from itself? This we may never know, but we can guess as to some reasons. Perhaps it is the very nature of the self-reflecting brain to question and fear its own potential? Perhaps fear is a tool used to hone the mind, to keep it sharp in a world where there may be challenges around every rock and corner? Perhaps— But I do believe that fear of reason and of thought is not innate in the minds of men.

Before I elucidate further on what use fear truly comes to, I feel that I must first discuss briefly the distinctions between two different kinds of fear. There is first instinctual "fear" (I hesitate to even call it so), the deep seated skepticism with which we view unknown or unknowable objects or sensations. This sense of "fear" is motivated by our desire to survive as an animal, and to prosper in life. When we tense or shudder at the roar of a bear, we are in essence attempting to process the sensations we are receiving so as to react to the situation. The bear is not in and of itself the object of fear so much as the potential harm to be done by the animal. This "fear" is a self-preserving agent, and largely beneficial in nature when applied to the real world and real challenges. We are able to use the information we receive to decide upon a course of action. The bear is roaring, but my eyes inform me that he is in a cage, and my memory tells me that cages keep those within from escaping to do me harm. Therefore I do not run, but I continue as if the bear where not there at all. And truly as a threat it is not there at all.

The other fear, the fear that I will be discussing and which concerns me most, is an imagined fear, and is, I believe, not innate, though it depends a great deal on the faculties of the former category of fear. This fear is in essence a form of irrational terror; terror at the unknown just for the sake of its being unknown. This fear can manifest itself in many ways, and often leads to a fear and hatred of those who are not innately afraid. The Terrorized cannot abide the idea of facing their fear alone, and must cultivate it in others. But, ah, this is where another human predilection comes into play; that of the desire for power and control. Why stop at cultivating fear? Why not use that fear to a personal advantage, namely the control of the individual whom fear is introduced to? Much could conceivably be gained by being the supplier of what is to be feared. Is not your own fear lessened when others fear along with you, and are you not comforted more when the other has more to fear then you? This is where faith can now safely enter the picture as a tool in what is essentially a terror campaign. "The fear of God" can be put into the minds of other men, and by being a Prophet (however fearful yourself) of that God you can prize from the situation a certain degree of power. Remember, God is seen as both a force one with nature and a force beyond nature.

This idea of a God has been used for some time to attempt to describe, explain, and justify our own existence. How and why this came about is not certain to me, but its having come about has led to many calamities in human consciousness and human affairs. Wars, hatred, and genocide are only some of the evil committed in the name of God. God controls all in the fearful mind, and he has the power to do ill or good to us at any juncture and for any, all, or no reasons. By extension, he who best understands how to engender a fear of God through faith can in the end control the minds and bodies of many men. We cannot see God, we cannot touch God, we cannot prove God, but we can project him onto what we can see, and touch, and prove. This is the capacity of faith to latch itself onto our capacity for reason, and you use that capacity like a drone for its own purposes. Reason is the idea that perhaps we do not need to fear something if we can attempt to understand it through empirical and intellectual means. Faith rejects this assumption, and posits in its place a cerebral tyranny that allows for no conceivable reality save that which justifies its own fear based assumptions. The fearful man will stoke fear in others for he is afraid of being afraid alone most of all.

Thus this fear of being alone can also play into the desire for power and control; we wish most to control what we most fear. Those who do not immediately join the Terrorized man in his terror are mistrusted, and are soon hated for this sin of being "braver" then they are. This dolt who lacks the fear of such an important man as he must lack something essentially human, or worse must disregard something in his nature out of nefarious impulses. He must protect himself from such inhuman men, and use any means necessary to do so, even in the face of rules set down by his God that proscribe against the very actions that must be taken to combat the enemy. God will forgive evils committed in furtherance of the interests of those who most revere him. Thus the man who imagines himself surrounded by fiends becomes a fiend himself to combat them.

There are many fiends to contend with indeed. The heretic is perhaps one of the most feared individuals for he has the capability to corrupt the rest of the group, and unbalance the scales of power in favor of himself at the expense of the prophet. The prophet must maintain his grasp on the fear of the multitudes or else he himself will be "no better" than them. The prophet is essentially a tyrant who could not come to power through normal political means. Think of this for a moment: is it not true that all the prophets of recorded time have been tyrannical in nature? If not in regards to the bodily realm then in the realm of the mind. What else could be construed from the tenants of faith except that the proscribed laws, thoughts, and morals that seek to bring an aspect of control over a society? Religious tenets to not exist in a political/societal vacuum. Even those rules that claim to seek greater redemption for the adherents give themselves away as tyrannical fiats by the very nature of the fact that they are rules at all. In a free society governed by humanistic laws there are always channels for redress or petition, even for those who violate the law. The law of God, the law of fear does not allow for such latitude. There is no place for exception, or challenge, let alone outright defiance within the court of divine dictate.

The power of the ultimate authority is invested within those who best understand the nature of the ultimate order; namely those who have most say in creating that order. These men (and it is almost without exception men), these prophets become prophets through their understanding of the word of the divine, the ultimate, the God. This understanding is essentially an expertise in fear, and how to channel it. What is more terrifying then unknowable, untouchable, unmovable authority, authority that allow no discontent because discontent *cannot be permitted*. It cannot, in truth, even be acknowledged to exist. But how then, if God does not permit such discontent, how then can it exist at all. This is where the genius of the purveyors of fear comes to full fruition. The notion of God comes with an equally universal notion of the good. And, good cannot exist without its antithesis: evil. The good is defined as that which comes closest to the universal concept that is God. God is good, good is God; these precepts will not, no, *cannot* be separated. If the good is God, then evil must be all that is not God. For this seemingly impossible state of affairs to exist one important principle must be circumscribed. This principle is perhaps one of the most insidious attacks on the rational human mind ever contrived: the principle of the bestowal of "free will" by God.

The connotations of the word "free" itself betray the nature of the will that follows from it. If the Webster's Ninth New Colligate Dictionary is to believed then the word "free" should be disassociated from all aspects of human ethics, reason, and thought. "Not determined by anything beyond its own nature or being: choosing or being able to choose for itself." This is as good of a definition of freedom as I have ever seen. To be free must be something beautiful to possess in the mind of a man. But, one must first be enslaved to be made free, and the condition can only be reached by the acquiescence of the master or the struggle and perseverance against the same on the part of the slave. "Exempt, relieved, or released from something unpleasant or *burdensome*".

      This sentence is importance in understanding the true nature of "free-will". God is a burden to those who think free: truly unobstructed and unrestrained thought and imagination cannot thrive or in truth exist within the strict boundries of God oriented faith. Those of faith give free will as an apology for, if not a condemnation of, the pursuit of thoughts and realities outside of the purview of God. Adam and Eve did not fall in spite of God, but in truth because of him. The apple was set aside as a token of absolute transcendence not to be comprehended by mere mortal serfs. The apple then was meant to be an object of fear; fear of ideas, fear of inquisitiveness, fear of comprehension in its most basic and primordial and human form. In this light we must understand that the tradition view of God must be turned on its head; God is a slave-master. A far reaching, paternal, and occasionally caring slave-master, but a slave-master known the less. To grasp the apple then is to grasp at the keys to the chains that bind many of us: fear forged, faith hardened, maintained by superstition and ritual. If God is a slave-master, who then is the snake? "You are not going to die, but God knows that as soon as you eat of it your eyes will be opened and you will be like divine beings who know good and bad." The words are said to be the cursed hiss of a fiendish serpent. Are they? Look at these words friends, and tell me that you do not see the reason in their meaning. Are we truly to believe that a fiend spoke these words? A villain who is the very antitheses of the good, the faith, the fear itself? If these be the words of snakes then we would all benefit from a serpentine education!

The Origin of Sin In the Western Mind

The end of faith and fear can only come about when the institutions that promote and use it are exposed for what they really are: parasites. Parasites prey upon the weaknesses of the host and feast upon its resources and fill it with poison. Faith is that poison, and fear is the vessel used to transport it. One of the most frequent users of this vessel is the Church. By "the Church" you can understand me to mean Christian power structures in particular and all religious institutions in general. Give me a Imam and I will show you a Priest, and give me a Priest and I will show you a Buddhist Monk etc.

In what is now commonly called "the post 9/11 era" many people have become much more aware of the historical realities of the Church in the past. The Crusades, the Inquisition, the persecution of Jews and "heretics", all of these things have come to the fore in the disparate arenas of popular culture, historical analysis, and perhaps more importantly politics. I believe that this period shows a disturbing trend towards greater abuse of fear as a tool to keep the "faithful" in line, and to influence the culture at large. For example The Catholic Church today inserts itself into almost every discussion about societal problems and scientific inquiry. Abortion, Stem cell research, evolutionary biology, the Holy See sees fit to share its esteemed opinions and beliefs with the public and with its political representatives. The leaders of the Catholic Church (and by the same token all religious institutions) claim to be the greatest example of human kindness, enlightenment and charity in the world. It is my contention that the Church is actually one of the worst offenders against human decency and reason in the world today.

According to Friedrich Nietzsche "Life is at an end where the 'kingdom of God' begins" (twilight of the idols, p. 55). If you were to ask the dearly departed Karol Wojtyla, nom de plume John Paul II, he would have a much different view. The Kingdom of God has dominion over our lives, indeed it is our lives. God is life and therefor there is literally no life without God. How do the esteemed fathers of the church know this? They are told directly because they communicate with the deity on our behalf of course. His holiness whom-ever-the-old-celibates-decide-is-the Pope also has the unexplainable, and down right amazing ability to infallibly speak on behalf of God. The problem is not so much that The Church has delusions of grandeur as it uses infantile arguments to justify these delusions. Translations of translations of translations of esoteric Hebrew theology and myth are said to be fact by so called experts who made up their minds about what they believe before they ever attempted a serious examination of their holy books. These "Theologians" (as they like to call themselves) and their apologists also employ faulty logic to create a foundation of "reason" for their odd beliefs. One of my favorite examples of this religious logic was employed by the conservative Christian Apologist Denesh D'Souza in a debate with the writer Christopher Hitchens. D'Souza made the ridiculous argument that Christians created the concept of Compassion. He backed up this erroneous declaration by citing the Biblical parable of the prodigal son. Hitchens tore this argument apart easily by pointing out that the story took place before there were any Christians at all: Jesus had not yet been crucified and St. Paul had not even been born yet. So D'Souza was undermined by his own belief system! Sadly, arguments like D'Souza's and other apologists are often excepted at face value by well- meaning people who have been trained and manipulated into believing such odd displays of "logic".

Religions treat their adherents like children. Like children believers learn to except and mimic whatever their elders and "betters" teach them. They were trained from a young age to look not for reason but for the absence of reason. The less logic inherent in a statement, the less provable the statement is, the more it is said to be valid and superior. Believers are expected to ignore and repress their own mental facilities and urges in favor of illogical fear (also known as faith). This is done for two reasons: to maintain power over the flock mentally and to protect themselves from the masses they have abused and stunted. Religion finds the basis of its beliefs in past fears superstitions and myths. These factors still influence the belief systems of Religion, but many of its tenants are now based upon reaction to issues that arose *since* the advent of the modern era.

These tenants are based upon innovations and progression in the realms of Sexuality and Procreation, Science, Philosophy, and the Secular world of Politics. Religion's reactions to these areas of human understanding and experience form the basis of the contemporary assault upon reason and intelligence. I hope to unveil to the fearful the perversions and the delusional beliefs of the church and how they impact their lives and their children's lives. These issues go far beyond molestation of children by priests. They influence the lives of human beings in a way that most do not understand, and sadly many never will. I will address these areas of concern one by one, and explain how the Church uses its tenants and beliefs to indoctrinate its members and keep them enthralled and in a constant state of fear. First however, to understand the special Religious concept of fear its twisted cousin sin must be explored.

The Wages of Sin

Original sin is the most disgusting and morally repugnant concept ever devised by human beings to torment themselves. The persistence of this massive falsehood is a stain upon humanity that can be blamed almost unequivocally upon religious faith in general but I will focus on the Roman Catholic Church in particular. The concept if Original sin can be blamed for hundreds of years of sexual repression and oppression. As the spawn of Adam's rib women where and (sadly) still are viewed as secondary creatures. The story of the fall of man is essentially a reactionary screed by men terrified and repulsed by women. The creed of Original Sin would become the central tenant of what would become Christianity. Why did this have to happen though? Why is sin so important to the reactionary forces that make up the Church?

According to the Catholic apologist Thomas Bokenkotter the concept of sin is not specifically outlined in the Old Testament. According to him there are at least four separate possible meanings of the word sin: "to violate a legal norm, to go astray, to rebel, to err" (Essential Catholicism, 295) . I believe that every one of these meanings places the act of sinning firmly within a "secular" and humanistic realm. By this understanding to sin would be to commit a crime against society. Societies throughout history have rejected those who distinguish themselves from the norm. This includes those who look different, speak differently, and *especially those think differently*. Therefore it is entirely possible for a person to rebel against a society without even meaning or wanting to have rebelled. To sin one needs only to be born physically or mentally different than those in power. Who were the power figures in the ancient middle east? Men of course! They (like all of us) were descended from a human species that had neither the time nor the reason to explore the world rationally.

These ancient forefathers lived their entire lives day to day. They lived in an environment that was brutal and unforgiving and they were constantly struggling to survive. This of course precious left precious little time for ration thought and observation. Everything was a potential threat so the world had to be seen through an entirely human lens. "The clouds in the sky are rumbling you say? Well it must be a great super human that is causing them to rumble. Now hurry up and help me skin this deer." Episodes like this may very well be the origin of faith-based thought. At the time this could have been little more than a side effect of constantly fluid existence. Humans soon transcended the hunter-gatherer life style however, and progressed to a more stable existence based around agriculture. This left more time for thought, but unfortunately it was no more rational then before. "That rumbling in the sky is often followed rain. We need rain to keep us alive!

Of course it must be caused by something, but not a human! It must be something much more powerful then you or I! If that is the case then we need to keep this powerful being happy and on our side." It is easy to criticize this mode of thinking today from a vantage point of expanded knowledge and understanding of the world and how it works. One of the worst mistakes we can make as reasonable thinkers is to take what we now know to be true and deride past peoples and societies for not knowing what we know. The knowledge we possess today was acquired in a enormous collective exploration of the world and reality. We did not have faith that we would learn what we now know: we had the will to learn it. It took millions of minds thousands of years of pain, struggle and persecution to get where we are today, and the truly amazing fact is that we are nowhere near the extent of our knowledge. We may have started looking at the world in mystical and anthropomorphic way, but as society evolved and became more stable our minds grew along at an explosive pace.

Admittedly it is rather difficult to reasonably interpret the world when your most pressing concern is finding something non-poisonous to eat. So if course it was predictable that our first impressions of reality would be somewhat... flawed. As society progressed however it became easier to abandon our old beliefs and misconceptions. Unfortunately human beings do not only love knowledge: the also love order and control. Flawed as it was our original prejudices obviously formed the foundations for the first societies. When building a shelter in a storm it is prudent to grab the supplies nearest at hand. In our species case this happened to be mythology and superstition. By a quirk in our nature (or out of evolutionary necessity) we humans always seem to produce individuals that desire to control and manipulate others. One of the best tools of manipulation has always been fear. Fear is both a wonderful motivator and nigh inescapable shackle. Humans use both physical and psychological forms of fear to control others. There are a few important difference between these two forms of fear however: a human employing physical forms of fear must constantly be on the lookout for other more powerful individuals. They might have to waste precious energy fighting an more powerful foe to retain control (and there is no telling what side your minions will choose to support).

Those who choose to employ psychological means of fear need only to outsmart any opponents. Also, a physical fear-monger can only control a group for as long as he retains his physical potency, which inevitably lessons with time and age. A psychological fear-monger however has only to keep his mental faculties at a reasonable level of potency in able to maintain control, and we all know it is much easier to remain smart then strong! This leads me to the greatest difference between the two forms of fear: the potential for alienating those who are subjected to the force that is fear. While it may seem much more affective to abuse and physically manipulate a child or weaker individual it in fact has the potential of giving the victim the anger and hate needed to wage a successful future challenge to the power structure that was so painstakingly built. On the other hand it is much more effective to teach a child or weak person to first fear you and then eventually fear themselves and their own minds. By using a universal moral code buttressed by a theological/mythological belief system it is possible to turn even the most physically healthy person into a quivering and mindless slave. To put it succinctly: Teach a man to fear your fist and you will control him for a season. Teach a man to fear his own mind and you can control him forever. And what is the term used to describe the fear of ones' own mind and body? It is sin.

"Free will" is its silly little cousin, used to justify and codify the former. If we were truly free from the power of God in the eyes of the prophets then we would undercut their own purpose. What slave-master loosens the chains of his own slaves for the betterment of their servitude? Either he is a master who has lost control, or a master who never had it. Or (and this possibility may truly set the minds of the fearful aflame with terror) perhaps the slave was never truly a slave after all? Perhaps the chains are imagined, the master a phantasm made up of smoke, delusion and apprehension. What then would be free then about our will? Nothing more then everything it already possessed. We are free, we were born free, we will always be free. The only unfree man is the man who indentures himself to fear. We should then talk of our being, our understanding, our potential, and not a will bound to anything but ourselves. We become more free every moment we allow ourselves to look upon the world, and contemplate what we see.

God is fear. Fear is manifested as Faith. Faith is enforced by Sin. Furthermore sin is a form of fear engineered by human minds to enslave and manipulate other human minds. Faith is a tool of those who are too afraid to see the world as a real thing. Faith is a denial of humanity out of fear of what that humanity might mean. Faith is a twisting of the human capacity for imagination. Faith is, was, and always will be a perversion of all that is human. Let us whisper this truth awhile amongst ourselves, and contemplate it. Do not fear this perversion: be grateful that is not a precondition of intellect and reason, and fight this disease with its only antidote: thought.

The Beauty of Thought and the Poverty of Belief

Kindly remember Socrates and his hemlock. He drank his frightful brew to show his fidelity to the laws of his nation, and to show his devotion to his ideals. When we remember Socrates (if we do at all anymore) it is as a martyr for the cause of reason and order. He was a prophet for a new age of thought and understanding; understanding that he need not pledge fealty to the brutal overlords that were theology and religious morality. The second was perhaps the more important as Socrates was not an atheist in name or action, but rather an ethical heretic in the eyes of those who appointed themselves protectors of the imagined moral purity of the youthful and the stupid. What was this affront to public decency? It was nothing less than the audacity to question the powerful and those who held claim to knowledge itself as an absolute certainty. Socrates rejected the idea that learned individuals could hold an absolute monopoly on the realm if speculation and in the end knowledge of the "truth". It seems Socrates rejected "truth" in all but its most fundamental sense; the asking of questions, the searching for answers were there are none or where none could easily be found, that is the realm of truth. Truly then, truth is in the act of searching itself. The question is the answer. The enlightened minds of Athens had a hard time excepting this, but then again how great in the end must the minds of self-aggrandizing polytheists be judged to be? This is a question for a greater mind then mine perhaps.

Socrates of course was not the absolute paragon of reason that he is often made out to be however. There were times when the great gadfly himself could not proceed without, as Nietzsche says, "[securing] support in the utterances of a divine voice" that supported the humble philosopher in his inquires and accusations. Thus even the most revered thinker in all of western thought (save perhaps that most unavoidable of moralists Christ) is in the end held in bondage to the idea that when in its time of direst need the human mind must surrender reason to faith. How then should we remember Socrates? As an infallible moralist and untouchable Philosophical wunderkind? Or perhaps he should be thought of as an irritable old fart who spent too much time drunk around the Delphic Shrine? I would declare that he is both, and perhaps neither. At his best

Socrates was a man who allowed himself to venture away from under the shadow that was religiously inspired fear and moral certitude in order to question why we must reside under such unwelcome shade at all. At his worst Socrates was a fearful man much like the leaders and pontificates who chose to martyr him. Socrates was a slave, like most of us were and are, but he did allow himself a glimpse into the hidden treasury that was his natural reasoned state. He is praised for this, if not quite revered.

Perhaps Socrates greatest gift to posterity (or perhaps it is in truth Plato's gift) is the idea that thought and reason itself should not be dismissed because it does not readily reveal immediate self-justifying truths and moral certitudes. Indeed I believe that we must go further still: thought and reason lead us *away* for absolute ideas and towards a better grasp of the natural flux of existence and circumstance. As soon as we allow ourselves to rest oh so leisurely upon our flat earths (or indeed our round ones!) we must remember that the solid ground we stand upon moves, and the endless sky we see is nothing but a dot upon a spot within a cloud of something so easily overlooked or never seen. Today's certainties are tomorrow's fairytales, and tomorrow's breakthroughs are yonder day's parlor talk. Or, this could not be the case at all, and we may choose to shackle ourselves blithely to a flat planet and stare at shadows in an imagined cave. Nothing comes without questioning. Nothing comes without thinking, and thinking is nothing without reason. Reason itself is not truth, nor is it even in and of itself correct by its very nature. Reason can lead to the most ridicules miscarriage or perversion of human potential. But, were reason has the potential for misuse, faith cannot bring anything but abuse and destruction upon the human mind and body. A reasoned man can choose to turn left or right; the faithful man cannot turn at all. Those who come to enlightened conclusions while adhering to faith do so in spite of their mental servitude; those who reach comparable conclusions through complete use of their human faculties do so without ever having to contemplate faith. They are in essence free; free to be what they are and what they strive to be.

Thought itself should not be set up as an idol. What we should marvel at is our capacity to think. Picture our mind as a river. This river feeds through its tributaries the great valleys and gardens that are the human psyche. Great fruits are born of these gardens, and treasures unfathomable are hidden within the valleys feed by the waters flowing through. What though should we think when we discover some within our midst who fear the river, and the mistrust the fruit born from its gardens? We do not know why they fear (nor truly do they), but they insist upon damming the flow so as to protect themselves from the imagined deadly potential of its current. "Of course" they lie, "the treasures and the gardens are beautiful and wonderful to behold. "But" (this most infernal of words) "But we must remember that which brings us this bounty may someday overflow its banks and drown us all." They declare this as truth, and in false concern for the well-being of others. They weep lying tears over the fate of the gardens and the river, but remember that they never liked the taste of the fruit! Using fear they move others to act with them. And thus the river is dammed for the good of the "safety" of our fellow men. The gardens starve, the treasures are unreachable in the parched valleys. Soon enough the people become restless and unhappy, and wish to seek the treasures and eat the fruits once more.

This is where the perfidy of the fear-mongers comes to full flower. They declare that the treasures hidden are best left unfound as they are nothing more than distractions that could lead us towards danger, perhaps there are even traps designed to ensnare us set by those who might do us harm. What is more, those who seek the treasure endanger us all with their recklessness, and of the fruits and gardens? They allow a bit of water through the dams to cultivate a garden of their own design, and thoroughly in their own control. This place is declared the only garden, and its fruits are much too sweet and tempting for the fearful populace. Their time and energy would better be spent avoiding danger, and taking every precaution to keep the status quo. This land is now fortress against themselves, a prison to protect its inmates from the imagined dangers without. This prison is named Eden, and its inmates are the potential within our human minds. The river is damned, and many reside within the prisons' walls. A few have breached the asylum walls and breathed the fresh free air, but too many still lie chained within. We see that there is nothing to fear, save for fear, and we should not waste ourselves with such roundabout concerns. It is up to those who choose to think to attempt to release the waters of our mind, and remove the dam from the river. Let us let the gardens grow once more. We deserve to seek its treasures and feast upon its fruit once again. There is no danger in thought, we have nothing to fear. We never have had anything to fear. To borrow the colorful words of the faithful, fear is a demon, and must be exorcized for us to live as healthy minds once more.

Art as Antithesis to Fear

What can be done to heal the damage wrought upon our minds by fear and faith? Are we doomed to live with the scars of our abuse at the hands of the terrorized for all of our existence? I believe not, and I have in my mind a few balms to sooth the burns inflicted by the wrath of God. The free expression of what lies in our minds would do much to heal our wounds. Our minds are living things that have the capacity to destroy, but also have an inverse power to create and innovate. Faith is in part the process of tearing down or suppressing the ability we have to think rationally and creatively. The obvious argument against this proposition is the traditional belief that religion inspired the greatest examples of art and rational thought. This is a well-constructed a widely believed lie. I have come to the conclusion through my experiences as an artist, as a thinker, and a rational person that all art and thought is a progression, a process of moving forward. Faith on the other hand is the act of staying still, anti-progression: faith is creative and rational paralysis. Consider a work of art traditionally seen as examples of religious and spiritual expression: the Ceiling of the Sistine Chapel as painted by Michelangelo. This great work was commissioned and financed by Pope Julius II to celebrate the glory of the Roman Church.

Michelangelo was indeed a devout Catholic, but the very work that made him a legend did so not because of the idea that his fresco glorified the stultifying absolutism of God. No, it was justly famous and in its own way venerated because of its embrace of *humanistic* elements inherent in its composition. Of course the bare subject matter is religious, but the context within which these religious episodes depicted are placed is entirely human and creative. When we look upon the part of the fresco that depicts God giving life to Adam do we marvel at the power and grandeur of the unwavering and all-powerful deity? Or do we admire the limp hand of Adam himself rising *upon its own power* towards an all too human depiction of the almighty? Michelangelo certainly did not mean to say with his painting that god had no part in creation.

That being said however we must not overlook the fact that the power of the composition comes from the humanity of the figures, and not from their cold deistic distance. We see the bodies of these beings contort, strain, flex, thrust, and move of their own volition and by their own power. When we see Eve looking out from the shadowy vortex that is God's cloak, we see an individual staring at Adam with true human compassion, interest, and perhaps even lust. Is not then god an mere supporting character, even an after though? If a rose by any other name smells as sweet, then can we not assert that Adam's reaching limb would be as profound against the back drop of an empty sky? Remember also that the very act of painting god was in itself a progression: the commandments of the wrathful deity himself forbid his puny creations from ever daring to depict him in "graven" form. Ironic that the very depiction of god is in essence a rejection of what god represents to those who revere and fear him.

Art is thought in its highest form, and thought is movement: movement away from assumptions and towards uncertainties and innovation. God is fear, and fear is stagnation: the stagnation of thought, the stagnation of rationality, the stagnation of contemplation in the face of the unknown.

For much of its existence humanity has stumbled about in the dark, metaphorically as well as literally. Fear in the form of religion and superstition was the only way to keep order in a world where creativity and deviation could spell doom and destruction for a group of huddled hunters in ice age chill. But eventually seeds were planted, roots laid, and imagination was one of the first crops that was able to grow. The fruit of this crop was art, and art manifested itself first not as a glorification of those tokens and deities that kept them comforted in a dark world. No, the first images depicted in a creative manner where the all too real things encountered in everyday life: a bison adorned with arrows from the hunt, a beautiful black manned horse, a flock of birds taking flight. All the more profound however was depiction of human things: a man with an erect phallus, a woman with a large full body and erotic features, things that organized religion would later tell us to revile and fear.

Perhaps the most touching and beautiful examples of this the earliest for of human imagination is the simple outline of a hand etched forever upon the wall of a cave. This hand is a monument to humanity, and serves to remind us that the there is nothing to be afraid of, nothing to hide from. There is nothing out to get us in the dark, and if we illuminate the world around us perhaps the most beautiful thing we will find is ourselves, and the mind that lets us contemplate the world. From the smallest bead to the largest Monument works of art are an affirmation of our place in the world, a physical realization of the concept that we are part of the world, and that the world itself is the most magnificent possibility. Who needs castles in the sky when we can walk amongst them here on earth? Only our fear prevents us from exploring the world, and shaping it through our thoughts and actions. Every moment we sit in contemplation of mighty faceless beings in the sky is a moment lost. Art is not a waste of time, but a celebration of time and our place within it, and an exploration and expression of existence. Religion and fear are the true waste: a waste of potential and a waste of life. What would the world be without art? A religious world. What would the world be without religion? A better world.

Whether you write, paint, sculpt, read, debate, draw, or contemplate you are creating art. Art is not an object: without art we would be stumbling blindly in the dark, unable to calm our fear, or sooth our unending pain and galling curiosity. Art is the anti-fear. Art is the light in the darkness. Art is our greatest potential realized. Of course art can liberate and inspire any mind, but it is often the case that artist who creates is often the artist who is vilified, hated, and tortured for his affront to fear. This is why so many artists have themselves given in to fear and faith: the creative mind is a powerful force but it takes a good deal of strength to stay free of fear, strength that many, by no fault of their own, do not possess. Remember it is the essential fact of human weakness in the face of the unknown that leads to fear and faith. It is equally true however that this all too human frailty can be harnessed towards the creation of magnificent and illuminating art. Imagination, creativity, reason, and art are potent antidotes to fear. Luckily for us these virtues come rather easily to a liberated mind. How though can a mind that has been shackled by fear for its whole existence be set free? Is it possible that some may have their capacity for free thought permanently stifled? Is there hope for the millions still imprisoned by faith and fear? Can they be brought from the darkness into the light?

Who are the Terrorized?

A revolution began in France when a prison was stormed. Those imprisoned were held to be the first freed from the tyranny that was the Absolute Monarchy in France. The revolution that exploded into life at the Bastille had been growing in the minds of enlightened men and women for decades, and had been growing in the hearts of the poor and voiceless for even longer. No longer would human beings be subject to the vociferous and unyielding whims of absolute rulers who claimed a mandate from an inscrutable deity. Reason and light would triumph over fear and darkness.

This revolution, when unleashed, spread across the whole world. It inspired the reinvention of new nations, the destruction of old national systems, and opened the floodgates allowing new ideas to rush forth. Many minds were freed in the years after the revolution and in the revolutions that followed. The French Revolution was no utopian ideal however. Many people died, and many of the ideals espoused were corrupted and misused. Again, perhaps inevitably for a society not yet used to exercising enlightened self-restraint and judgement, the germ of fear was allowed into the mix and this did no small amount of damage to a humanist and liberal crusade for justice. However, the freedom that sprung forth outweighed the damage done in its name. At times extremism, disobedience, and on occasion even violence are inevitable, if regrettable, necessities on the road to freeing those poor minds and bodies that are enslaved by fear and the fearful. The Ancien Regime feel, and while it attempted to revive itself a few time over the next few centuries, it could no longer take hold as it once did: without debate and without resistance.

Thankfully such violence is not often needed. A new revolution is brewing in the minds of a new generation of the oppressed, the fearful, and the enlightened. This revolution will not attempt the overthrow a rotten system of government, but an entire perverted mode of thought: faith in a god and all that this implies about the ways humans must therefore think and behave. And it will be done not with muskets, barricades or execution devices, but with the more enlightened and in the end more potent weapons of reason, science, kindness, and imagination.

I have already outlined how and why I believe fear, through faith, destroys our potential as human beings. Now we must explore how to emancipate the terrorized masses still enslaved. Perhaps the best way to begin the process of emancipation is to start young, so to speak. Children and young adults are the silent victims of the scourge of faith. Every day children are ritualistically abused, mentally stunted, and intellectually insulted. Every circumcised boy or girl is a victim, every child told his body is a dirty thing is a victim, every young person told to fear that which is new and innovative is a victim. You are a victim. I am a victim. And yet, the saddest truth is that you are most likely a victimizer as well. Those preyed upon are the most likely to prey upon others, whether consciously or not. Children are natural thinkers; the very nature of their minds dictates that they doubt, explore, and question the world and ideas around them. We must respect and nurture this instinct. The last thing we should do is suppress it with stories meant to impair the ration capacities of young minds. This is of course the aim of childhood religious indoctrination.

The truly fearful, and by this I mean the truly religious, do not want to rear children who question the basic tenants of the faith in which they grew up. From an early age many children are numbed by asinine religious fables and subtly terrified by being told that are essentially evil creatures by the nature of their own births. What could be more chilling to a child then the prospect that they are in some way "bad"? In truth, there are very few things that sadden me more than the sight of a child walking out of a church. Religious teaching can only damage young minds. They are told that science is not to be trusted, that it is more important to pay lip service to an invisible overlord then to reasonably relate to the real world. Even something as simple as the concept of a theory is twisted: Evolution is *only* a theory and this they are told makes it all the less credible. These are only small symptoms of a disease that has plagued our society since its beguiling. The disease is past down from generation to generation, violently pounded into the minds of the impressionable. Whether we are aware of it or not the truth remains: we are intellectually raping our children. Every page of scripture is another link in the chain that imprisons the true nature and potential of the world's youngest thinkers. This must end. We must end this cycle, and free the human species from the bounds of fear.

Who Are The Free?

      The Free of this world are an amorphous group, ever changing and ever expanding, with some lapsing into fear in moments of human weakness. It is not always easy to combat systems created by human minds that are designed to find patterns and things to fear in even the most innocuous of situations. There is are still many people out there, intelligent, potentially brilliant people, who are trapped within the systems of mind and culture that they were born into. There is hope however within the maw of idiocy and darkness. There are freemen scattered amongst the prisoners: these are the freethinkers the men and women who have not been enslaved by fear. Freethinkers are grocery clerks, petshop owners, footballers and highschool students. Fortunately the freethinkers are also teachers, and parents and leaders and writers and artists. This is more than enough to sow the seeds of the downfall of fear and faith. The freethinkers are a diverse group of individualistic minds. Perhaps the most outspoken and freest minds among them are the atheists. The atheists completely reject the pernicious idea of a god or universal moral force that controls all of existence. The atheists do not allow themselves to be enthralled by the fanciful and ridicules machinations of the terrorized. The atheists are the only truly free people left on earth. They are a small minority of the general human population, but as a whole they represent perhaps the last best hope for our collective liberation from fear. The atheists did not ask for this burden, but they will accept it out of their profound love for humanity. Atheists love humanity because they themselves are human: there need not be any other reason than this. The atheists do not believe we share a common soul, a common debt to a sacrificial god, a common sin. What the atheists believe we share is life in its most pure and simple form. We share the distinction of being living beings, and atheists believe that this is enough to justify mutual understanding and cooperation towards a greater good.

      This good does not lie in transcending our lives in search of a nebulous after-realm, but in embracing the only true life we will ever have. Fear is a waste of human life. We cannot afford to waste one moment in terror. We must embrace the reality of our existence and immerse ourselves in its full spectrum of beauty, ugliness, color, and chaos. Life is for living; the opposite is to live in fear of life. Every time I open my eyes I want to see something new. I want to experience everything I can sense. I want to think, to use my incredible mind to create and to innovate. A mind is a tool for change. If it is not used as such then it is nothing more than a lump of grey tissue. Millions of people in the world today live their lives with this lump between their ears and never realizing that all they have to do to revive it is to think. The terrorized hold all of the keys to the cells, but they choose not to see them, and in many cases they cannot see them. The free-thinkers, and especially the atheists have the power to show the terrorized that they hold these keys, and that they can join the ranks of the blissfully free. What must the terrorized do to become free? They must reject the idea of a god given freewill, they must reject the idea of sin, they must reject the idea of blind faith, they must reject the idea of an earned afterlife, and most of all they must reject the idea of a god. There is no other way to free the terrorized and the fearful.

Before you attack your enemy you must identify him, and understand his motivations and beliefs. You must identify his strengths and weaknesses. What follows is an essay in which I will address the idea of faith and fear and outline its faults, failings and evils. I am not an expert in any of the fields I have discussed. I am at best an interested observer, amateur historian, political activist, and a writer. This essay will not be a comprehensive study of the subject, and I expect that many people will have their own opinions about what I write. For the most part I will be addressing certain issues within the subject I am addressing, and not a general historical and encyclopedic treatment of it. What I can promise you is that I will write truthfully and site every word that I use from another source. Anyone who disputes the words and views I present can check the source for themselves. My goal is simply to help people. I hope that someday a child can be born into this world without having to be a slave to the fear and hate that has doomed so many in our history to sad and painful lives. If I can reach one person and help them see the world through fearless eyes then I will have accomplished something that I can take pride in.

Rebellion Against Metaphysical Tyranny

There are times during my day when I feel an overpowering feeling of malaise and depression. I feel that I am powerless before an idea that I never subscribed to nor believed: that there is a God who rules this world and all others and It is he who dictates to use our own morality and meaning. I live in a little apartment in a little cold part of my enormous country that exists as a fortress of faith within a world that persists to believe. This is quite a lonely feeling. It is a lonely feeling, but an oddly pleasant feeling also. During the dark ages Muslim Scholars and, to a lesser extent, Christian Monks kept alive the knowledge and the wisdom humans had acquired during the Greek and Roman times. These two ancient peoples had defied the fear that permeated their world and culture and explored the potential of their minds and the natural world. The had a grasp of science, philosophy and art that was not equaled until the Enlightenment, and in many ways has never been matched. Alas, this period of young and growing reason would not last. Some remarkable individuals within the Mediterranean community had been able to combat the evil of the invisible tyranny that was slowly being unleashed upon the world from isolated enclaves in the Middle East. The Romans did not have the fortitude of their Greek forbearers and it was they who succumbed to monotheism.

This philosophy is perhaps the most destructive and obscene mode of thought ever unleashed by human beings upon human beings. Before the introduction of monotheism there had been deity worship, but this worship was connected in real way with the basic naturalism and humanity of humans and their modes of living. The gods were mere supermen who saw fit to make themselves seen and felt only when asked, summoned, or during natural processes. The minds of people were enslaved by these supermen, but this was a kinder slavery then that which was soon to come. Monotheism unleashed universal existential tyranny upon the world. No more was it enough to be alive and human, happy and sad, alive or dead. It was now a matter of unquestionable obedience and perpetual terror in exchange for a utopian and unquantifiable future amidst the clouds and the perpetual companionship of the tyrant who dictated the terms of their existence. God was not a god. God was existence itself. The love you felt, the hate you had, the intelligence you possessed was meaningless if not seen to be one with the unknowable of the invisible godhead.

It was not enough to live anymore. One had to live for a purpose other than himself and his fellow man. He had to live for the glory and the pleasure of a petty desert demon that had somehow maneuvered itself into the Imperial crown of all existence. Slavery took on a more violent and numbing meaning. Submission was the greatest moral act, and self-denial was the price that must be paid to achieve this feat of eternal fealty. One must scourge and belittle his own humanity and the bow on a bed of thorns and thank the sky for the privilege. We became nothing but dumb puppets on a string that did not exist but could not be denied. We lost our humanity to this plague and we have yet to regain it as a whole species. The free of thought and body ran from the horrible fortress of theocracy and hid forever in the forest where they could perchance find a humble sanctuary for their dreams and ideas.

One of these sanctuaries is the cold little apartment that I spoke to you of earlier. I reject the Invisible Tyranny, but I am in no way untouched by it. I must live in its shadow every morning I wake. I am of course not the first to be galled by the shadow of the imaginary monster. Many of our greatest minds and fellow men were destroyed by wrath of the tyrant. I do not count myself as an equal in intellect and impact to the individuals I will list, but I do feel a share a common purpose with them. Galileo dared to look at the stars and wonder, and he was shut away like a mental patient. I hold myself in solidarity with him; who but a tyrant *would* command us to forgo the use of the minds that make us oh so human? Was not YHWH our Prometheus? We are his creation yes? His pride and joy? Was it not he who gave us fire? Was it not he who wanted us to grow? Was Prometheus ashamed with his clay playthings? This was not the case. Prometheus should not be stained by association with such a fiend as YHWH. No, our glorious creator is more akin to that insipid brother Epimetheus. That insolent fool created nothing but shame and chaos. We are not his creations but his concubine: we are the brides of ignorance. We are little Pandora's. Our Epimetheus forbid us from indulging our natural inquisitiveness, and told us that there were terrible daemons in the box entrusted to him. He wanted us to live in terrible pitiful ignorance of the truth and of reality no matter how hideous or galling. We wisely ignored him and we opened the box and let the daemons out. This box is of course a crude metaphor for the fleshy little box between our shoulders.

There can indeed be horrendous consequences when humans think, but it is equally true that infinitely more terrible things can occur when they choose not to. So much good can potentially arise from simple human thought: Galileo was just a man trying to exercise his humanity, but of course that is enough for the fearful servants of the almighty. At least Galileo shares a fate in common with other great humans: Socrates was martyred because he dared to question anything and everything; De Sade was imprisoned and tortured like a feral beast for daring to explore our beautifully crude and crudely beautiful bodies and their desires; Diderot was despised for his lyricism because it did not derive from the divine; Nietzsche would be vilified because he dared to question the values that we frame our entire lives around; Lewis Carroll was ground to a spineless pulp by the guilt that derived from his fear. Countless other famous personages and millions of other obscure somebody's where abused and denied their dignity by the tyrant and his courtiers.

Think of it: we are the only species that enslaves itself at the whim of itself for the simple fact that once upon a time we were afraid of the world that gave us birth! We are poor neurotic little things! We never saw fit to wean ourselves off of the intoxicating but poisonous milk that we thought we needed to get through the rough and scary times. We are now by no means masters of our world, but are we not a little closer to at least understanding that the clouds to not hide angry giants and the earth does not hold within it bowels the vengeful dead? Are we still so meek and terrified as to be cowed by our own shadows? Or do we not even recognize the shadows as our own? The tyrant does seem to cast a long silhouette, even if it is an erroneous one. I look about me every day and see people I care for, respect, and love cast into darkness by the fears that derive from their own thoughts. So many torture themselves needlessly! Oh how I weep for the poor minds who cast themselves into the streets and flagellate themselves to appease a King who does not even exist! Even the best of us, the most wise, those of us who *should know better* feel the bit of the flail.

The tyrant is a cruel taskmaster and he brokers no defiance or deviation from his rules and from his almighty will. When I see great men and women grovel on their knees and apologize for their own human talents and their human needs and their human thoughts I also feel a touch of the lash. There is nothing more painful to behold then the humiliation of those who you most admire. I love these people as I love myself even though they were amongst the fearful, and I forgive the childish fear and naïveté even they at times displayed. A fitting epitaph for these poor wretches is hard to arrive at. What words can properly commemorate the sacrifice of our best humanity upon an altar of fear and self-hatred? I do not claim to have the words within me to honor them, but I will share a phrase that I feel sums up the condition many of my fellow humans live and die in.

Victor Hugo wrote of a Bishop and an old revolutionary in his great tome *Les Miserables.* The Bishop came to save the soul of the decrepit old liberal. The man had fought for freedom from fear and tyranny his whole life, and has used his mind and his body to the utmost to achieve a measure of dignity in an undignified world. By doing so he of course had to rebel against the tyrants both existential and imagined. As is the case with so many others though this breathing monument to human potential was eventually overcome by his own fear of the great unknown: death reared its subtle head and suddenly the revolutionary succumbed to the fear that had been drilled into him by society. The Bishop came for his confession and the Revolutionary was on the verge of giving in… And yet a last bit of resolve entered his conscience and he used his dying breaths not to recite a tortured apology for his own existence but a poignant and tragic declaration of fear mixed with defiance. What was this thing that held so much sway over his mind and heart was it truly there? What was this terrible god? And then it came to him. He turned to the priest and cried:

"The infinite exists. It is there. If the infinite had no me, the me would be its limit; it would not be infinite; in other words it would not be. But it is. Then it has a me. This me of the infinite is God. "

With this he expired, so close to grasping the truth that he and his real world brothers and sisters failed to see: *We are the infinite! We are what we fear! We are the fount of our own meaning! We are the heirs to our own destiny! We are the righteous and the wretched! We are nothing more than what we make of ourselves!*

We are everything that we make ourselves out to be! We are God!

Thus our great Epimetheus can be revealed for what he (it) really is: a fraud of the highest order… And an illusionary one at that!

Perversion?

Faith is the worst Perversion. The faithful are thus the most perverted amongst us. I have talked about how humanity as a collective unit has suffered fear and faith. I will now talk about our individual experiences and culpability. I will play Socrates for a moment and ask what then is "perversion"? The fearful would have us believe that perversion is a condition of the soul, the heart, and the mind. It is a contaminant and a disease that must be cut bleeding from the holy body. We are told that those who do not fear God are perverted. By fear we must understand that they mean faith, and by faith we should read obedience. We must obey the laws of the tyrant god to the letter and without even a hint of a thought of deviation. *He* gave us life and we must obey! He gave our existence meaning and we should obey! We want to make it to heaven yes? An evil heart, a perverted soul cannot ever reach the endless glory that is heaven! We are told that everything that we do not understand is by its very nature perverted. Man shall not lie with man… but he may condemn himself to a loveless passion-less life that shuns human contact and helps to breed perversion. A woman must not sacrifice her holy gift of virginity… but her father can give her to a crowd of horny old men to be gang raped in place of his male guests. The pit awaits all who do not crawl on bloody knees to the thrown of the coming Lord, or to the feet of the Lost Imam, or to the glaring maw of the black whole of self-denial known as Nirvana. Fear is a weapon for those who will not think. It is a double-edged sword though. Those who wield it risk cutting themselves as deeply as those they wish to smite. Those who live in fear never experience life as it truly is: what we perceive it to be with our remarkable senses and imagination. We can shape the world with our eyes and our minds… Of course there are moments of pain and panic and desperation, but this comes with *living*. We are organisms that have evolved slowly over time. Natural selection is no kind "mother nature" or creator god. It is a process fueled by necessity and inexorable, inevitable, endless change. We are told by the fearful that this is a most terrible blasphemy. God created all things, and only through God can meaning be arrived at. We are lepers to them, we unbelievers. We must not allow our evil arguments to contaminate their precious little slaves/children. Ironic that the fearful always laugh and call our arguments "weak" and "obviously flawed" but when we actually start to talk to someone who will listen with unplugged ears they get uneasy and decide that isolation is the better part of valor. The round up their little disciples and hide them away in a warm little place where they can drink their poison in peace and quiet. Thus they are deeply cut to the quick by their own fear, though they would never recognize that they were injured.

Children are natural detectives in regards to the world. The fearful would have them go their whole lives without asking any questions of themselves, their elders, and the world. And we are supposed to see virtue in this? Is it not something of a perversion to deny a growing mind the food of thought it needs to grow? What is more beautiful to the religious mind then a child being sent against his will to confirmation. This is not a regretful abusive event to the fearful: it is indeed necessary to preserve the everlasting glory of God! Never mind that to force a child to pledge his heart and his mind to something he does not understand and perhaps does not want to is a *perversion* of the purpose and potential of his mind. Never mind that it probably means nothing to him, and his "faith" will only acquire meaning as he is slowly and methodically terrorized using his own thoughts and human urges as a specter of unspeakable evil. Never mind all of that: it must be done to save the child: Forgive this poor little doubter Father! He knows not how to not think!

Sam Harris, Dawkins, and other atheist activists have said that religion is something of an intellectual and emotional failing of the human race. For example Dawkins has said that

Many of us saw religion as harmless nonsense. Beliefs might lack all supporting evidence but, we thought, if people needed a crutch for consolation, where's the harm? September 11th changed all that.

I would agree with the basic substance of this paragraph, but I would go even further. September 11th changed nothing that was not already apparent to anyone with any sense of ethical and mental clarity. What the Muslim radicals did that day was nothing. It was NOTHING compared to the cumulative damage done by everyday people in everyday places against everyday people in everyday ways. We are told to despise our bodies, our minds, our culture, our neighbors, our friends, family. And all of this is done on an everyday, hour by hour, moment by moment basis! Every *second* of our lives is a continuing terror attack upon our senses and our sensibilities as human beings. If the fearful truly chose to think then they would realize that what happened on that autumn Tuesday was nothing more out of the ordinary or sinister then what happens on any other given day in the world. Go into any Catholic Church and you will see people standing in line to eat a cracker they *truly believe* is the body of a living/dead Hebrew faith-healer. Go into any Buddhist Temple and you will find scores of individuals attempting to surrender their own feelings and emotions in a nihilistic attempt to emulate an ancient Indian "Dead-Beat Dad". For that matter go into almost any home on the face of this earth and you will see families devoting their time, energy and emotions to thanking an invisible daemon for giving them the things that they themselves earned by the sweat of their own brows! These acts and ideas are no crutch! They are not harmless! They are a moral and ethical choice made by otherwise sane and well-adjusted adults and forced upon the still emerging consciousness of children. When taken together I see what, for example, Christians do on Sundays no more or less destructive or evil then what Muhammad Atta and his cohorts did on Tuesday the 11th of September. Both had a choice to make as *adults*. They chose to deny their humanity and to deny the real world in favor of an illusory and simplistic nether realm ruled by a tyrant who does not exist, never existed, and furthermore *should not exist!* They are morally culpable for the pain their actions have caused to anyone and everyone. They are the perverted ones, the fearful, the faithful. Not the Free.

What Now?

      What then can we say conclusively about Faith and Fear as it exists today? It is still strong and still consuming lives as we speak, and it shows no signs of finally disappearing from this world. That being said there is some hope; more human beings than ever before are realizing that the world does not freeze on its axis when God is removed as the primary mover. There are countless thousands of human beings being born into families that do not feel it is their duty to warp and terrorize the minds of their offspring to continue a tradition of metaphysical servitude. The fear that is inherent to religious faith to this day is in large part due to the fact that the religious institutions and systems that we have deal with on a day to day basis have their origins in societies in the past where illiterate men, women and children were compelled to believe by example and by moral terror. It is the antithesis of reason to believe something based on what an authority figure drills into you with guilt, emotional manipulation, and hackneyed and moralistic fables. It is hard to escape fear and faith when you do not even have the ability to read the sources of the faith and superstitious rituals you are force fed! The good thing is that "believers" are more canny than ever, or at least they have the potential to be. The United States has tens of millions of people who no longer belong to a religion or creed, and millions more atheists and agnostics who have taken the final step out of fear and the first step in to exploring themselves and their world without faith in unknowable and terrifying absolutes to hold them back.

      That is not to say that there are no enclaves left in the world where illiteracy, general superstition and/or theocratic elites keep thousands if not millions in the dark and afraid, but there is now the potential to reach even those who used to be written off as unreachable. As we see in the Asia, in Europe, and slowly, ever so slowly, in the Middle East and Africa there is a burgeoning renaissance of free-thought and skeptical inquiry. It is not far-fetched to believe anymore that the next great rational philosopher, groundbreaking scientist or mind expanding artist will come from what is called the "third world". In fact I would go so far as to say that it is inevitable that rational thought and skepticism will find a wonderful home in the cradle of the world civilizations. We can only hope.

Until then we can work for a better less fearful future and do our best to be advocates and examples for a life lived without faith in God or absolute blind moral systems. Truth is an important but misunderstood aspect of humanity and humanism. Truth is not a fact or a figure but a way of living and a mode of thought that does not allow for anything but the fullest exploration, protection and expression of human life and potential. Truth is not an ideal or an artifact of universal meaning. It is instead a way to look at the world that does not interfere with the human need to understand and to imagine our world and the potential of New Worlds. We do not need prophets or seers or messiahs to lead us into a new world. We only need only look to each other and into ourselves. For it is in the human mind that the best hope of the world lies, and where the last redoubt against fear and faith continues to persevere and grow more resilient.